Hilaire Belloc

by
Karl Schmude

*All booklets are published thanks to the
generous support of the members of the
Catholic Truth Society*

CATHOLIC TRUTH SOCIETY
PUBLISHERS TO THE HOLY SEE

Contents

Dedicated to the memory of my father, A.J. Schmude, whose Bellocian courage and courtesy remain the permanent inspiration of a grateful son.

This booklet is a revised version of *Hilaire Belloc: His Life and Legacy*, by Karl Schmude, published by the Australian Catholic Truth Society (Melbourne, 1978).

Belloc's Influence

"The other day, in a curiously moving country church at West Grinstead, we laid to rest, not without the tears of memory, an old and tired man. It was a funeral of circumstance; the Mass was Pontifical, the habits of many religious Orders graced the sanctuary, and schoolboys' voices lent an intolerable beauty to the *Dies Irae*. But in essence it was a country affair; some of Hilaire Belloc's friends had met to see his body lowered into the grave – there, in Sussex earth; there, beside the wife he had so long mourned; there, with the house he had lived in for forty years, till it became 'like a bear's fur' to him, only a few miles away. Today, as if humouring that other side of him, which loved stateliness and the just proportion of well-ordered things, we gather with muffled footfalls among the echoing vaults of a great cathedral – we, lesser men, who have lived so long under the shadow of his championship, to remind ourselves what it is we have lost, and to do him honour."[1]

In such words did Mgr Ronald Knox inaugurate his tribute to Hilaire Belloc, in the panegyric he preached at Westminster Cathedral on 5th August, 1953. The visible life of a great and formidable figure had ended, but Mgr. Knox stressed the invisible grandeur of immortality.

For those living more than half a century after Belloc's death, that immortality has yet to acquire any visible or earthly dimension. Belloc has declined in favour, not only among the general reading public which accorded him fame in his lifetime, but even in the Catholic community which he did so much to shape and strengthen. His life and writings have drifted into the coves of historical memory, and even commemorative activities, such as on the centenary of his birth in 1970 or on the 50th anniversary of his death in 2003[2], have done little to resurrect his name.

To a large degree the fading of Belloc's influence is not difficult to explain. He has experienced the customary eclipse of all authors immediately after their death; and, indeed, unless a writer happens to be concerned prematurely with a matter that subsequently seizes widespread attention – as, for example, George Orwell was with the nature and effects of totalitarianism – he is unlikely to escape this trough of posthumous neglect.

In Belloc's case, his reputation has also suffered severely from the tides of social and religious change. The world he inhabited was centred upon Europe, the faith he proclaimed was centred upon France. It is in different directions that the eyes of our present generation are turned; within a global rather than European environment that the destinies of our time are chiefly being played out.

European and Universal

Belloc was, avowedly and profoundly, a European. In H.G.
Wells's curt epigram, he appeared to have been born all
over Europe. Certainly his ancestry was a rich and unusual
amalgam of French, English and Irish influences. He was
born in France on 27th July, 1870; his father was a French
barrister and his mother an Englishwoman who figured in
the early suffragette movement; his paternal grandfather
had married the daughter of an Irish Colonel who was in
the service of the French Crown. When Belloc was fairly
young, the family moved to England, where his formal
education took place. He was enrolled in 1880 at the
Oratory School at Edgbaston near Birmingham – which
still bore the stamp of its celebrated founder, Cardinal
Newman – and he graduated in 1887 with high distinction.
Thenceforward, he spent most of his life in England –
undergoing naturalisation in 1902 – although his love of
Europe and his passion for travel took him at frequent
intervals to the Continent.

Citizen of Christendom

But Belloc was not merely a citizen of Europe: he was
above all a citizen of Christendom, of a Europe shaped in

the crucible of the Catholic faith. At an early stage, he gave expression to this citizenship:

> "I desire you to remember that we are Europe; we are a great people. The faith is not an accident among us, nor an imposition, nor a garment; it is bone of our bone and flesh of our flesh: it is a philosophy made by and making ourselves. We have adorned, explained, enlarged it; we have given it visible form. This is the service we Europeans have done to God. In return He has made us Christians."[3]

For the Catholic people, the recent decades of religious and cultural turmoil present a timely opportunity for reviewing Belloc's life and achievement. There is now an imperative need for the clarifying vision of a great Catholic mind; the spiritual penetration of a deep and authentic faith; the divine wisdom of an integrated Christian humanism. To an eminent degree, Hilaire Belloc fulfils the dimensions and demands of such a universal vocation.

Historic faith

Most insistently does he serve to bring the Catholic consciousness face-to-face with its past, in the way that Pope Benedict XVI is projecting to the people of a new century. Since the 1960s, there has been a profound tendency to discount the historical character and continuity of Catholicism, and to promote a compulsive spirit of escape from the Catholic past; in particular the period immediately pre-conciliar, as if this period were too benighted to qualify as part of salvation history. This tendency created a psychological barrier to any balanced understanding of the Catholic tradition, and resulted in a sudden loss of meaning and identity. Now a new generation has emerged, especially in the secularised West, which is showing fresh interest in the perennial faith of the Church. The rise of different movements of evangelisation, and the new surges of popular Catholicism such as World Youth Day, have begun to challenge the habit of shunning and even suppressing the historic faith of the Catholic people. Such trends are gathering force, and they reflect an outpouring of imaginative sympathy for the people we have historically been.

English-speaking Catholicism

Few individuals could supply a better channel of access than Belloc to the Catholic tradition in all its richness and vitality. "More than any other man," declared Frank Sheed, "Belloc made the English-speaking Catholic world in which all of us live."[4] He it was who challenged the social climate under which Catholics suffered, and who inspired them with a new confidence in the power and grandeur of their faith. He it was who, by means of a vital scholarship and vision, elevated and enhanced the intellectual standing of that faith. To look again at the person and mind of Belloc is to catch a glimpse of the Catholic tradition under challenge. It is to offer a salutary insight into our recent past and a vivid conception of our historical experience.

No doubt it is now difficult to evoke the memory of siege and encirclement that marked English-speaking Catholics of an earlier generation – and to appreciate the enthusiasm of relief and thanksgiving with which they welcomed Belloc, not only in England but also in countries as distant as Australia. My father, A.J. Schmude, was an early member of the Campion Society, a lay association formed in 1931, in honour of the Oxford scholar and martyr St Edmund Campion, to provide higher education for young Australian Catholics. My father always recalled with spontaneous gratitude the sense of excitement and resolution which Belloc's writings inspired among Australian Campions. As one Catholic journalist, Frank Murphy, recalled:

> "It is sober fact that the lively growth of Catholic Action, or the Lay Apostolate, in Australia goes back to the meetings of the Campion Society in Melbourne, in the early thirties, when young Catholic men, to meet the secularist challenge of their day wrestled with its problems in groups formed of their own initiative and which were adult education at its best ... They read

widely and they read Belloc. Not every Campion worshipped the man, but those who did made their voices heard, taking on something of his power. There is no doubt of his influence."[5]

Pioneer against intolerance

Here stood a man who could not be disregarded; whose personality and prophetic insight could not be ignored or dismissed. In a social atmosphere of supposedly greater tolerance, it is, perhaps, complacently easy to regard Belloc's style of championship as sharply unappealing and even harmful. Yet this would be to read history backwards and to apply to another age our own more yielding standards of judgement: it would be to assume that Belloc's importance for the Catholic people was only intellectual, and to neglect the enormous psychological benefit of his arrival. As Christopher Hollis observed:

"It is true that we have now moved into an ecumenical age in which it is the fashion to speak with all courtesy of those who differ from us and in which we can with confidence look for fair-mindedness from them in return. All that is to be welcomed, but, if we feel inclined to criticise Belloc for not writing in that manner, it is necessary to remember what was the confidently Protestant English mentality of Victorian times, what was the language in which it was then the fashion to speak of Catholic beliefs, and we may then understand how it was perhaps necessary to challenge that world with a gesture of bravado in order to break down its self-confidence. If the modern Catholic writers can write to an audience from which they can confidently expect to receive fair play and can address it in moderate terms, it is largely because Belloc in his time breached for them the wall through which they can enter as perfect gentlemen and without a ruffle to the parting of their hair."[6]

Model of the faithful servant

In decisive ways, Belloc remains to this day a powerful exemplar of mainstream Catholicism – a towering testimony to the kind of historical people we are, and the kind of tradition to which we are heir. His way of being Catholic – the incarnational way, radical and traditional, firm and forgiving, confident and humble, realistic and hopeful, obedient and free – stands as the central and compelling model of a faithful servant.[7]

Yet the attraction of Belloc has never been restricted to Catholics. Many of his own friends did not share his religious beliefs – among them, the diplomat and author, Duff Cooper, who said: "I disagree with Belloc over nearly everything, but he is one of my greatest friends."[8] Again, his work has not been of interest merely to fellow-

Catholics: it has tended to have immediate appeal to the young regardless of their religious background. The English social critic, Bernard Levin, who was of Jewish descent, warmly remembered his adolescent impressions of Belloc and of Chesterton. He recalled how "enthralled, stirred and delighted" he was by their writings, which were "immediately intelligible to a schoolboy," for they "spoke of rebellion, and non-conformity, and romanticism...". Belloc and Chesterton, continued Levin, "battled for their creed in fair weather and foul and command one's respect alike by their skill and valour in the battle and the gay certainty of their convictions."[9]

Sympathetic sceptic

Apart from his ardent and romantic side, Belloc also possessed a native scepticism. "By my nature," he once confided to a friend, "I am all sceptical and sensual – so much so as hardly to understand how others believe unseen things or do violence to their inclinations."[10] Temperamentally, as Robert Speaight pointed out, Belloc was a child not of the Age of Faith, but of the Age of Reason; he himself was tempted by the questionings of the 18th-century Enlightenment. The total rejection of the Christian claim by a sceptic was a mood he always understood. It was, finally, the only serious challenge – one which the naturally devout may be apt to discount, but which, for most people, has always been the supreme temptation; epitomised forever in Christ's own desperate cry from the Cross to the God who had forsaken him – the instant, as G.K. Chesterton commented, when even God Himself almost became an atheist. As Christopher Hollis noted of Belloc:

> "Increasingly as he grew older, he came to see that whether we survive or not life was essentially about death. The question of what happens at death was the one question of real importance. He had no inborn sense of survival. The world around him bore in itself all too few marks that it was the entrance hall to a truer reality beyond itself. He was quite open to the sceptical fear that nothing was true at all."[11]

In his writings, Belloc addressed again and again this greatest of challenges. In 1938, he produced a short book, *The Question and the Answer*, which was a lucid presentation of the Catholic answer to the central question of human existence, "What am I?"

Preparation for Public Life

It is not necessary to accept Belloc wholly or uncritically in order to appreciate and honour his principal achievements; just as it is not necessary, or even desirable, to favour a total return to a vanished Catholic past in order to appreciate and recover its permanent traditions.

Military background

Belloc was a forthright and uncompromising man whose outlook and style are now decidedly out of fashion. At the age of four, in a letter to his sister, Marie Belloc Lowndes, he wrote: "I have a drum but I'm not allowed to beat in the house, only in the garden or out in the road."[12] In adult life he was indeed to beat it "out in the road" – loudly and commandingly. The literary critic, Desmond MacCarthy, likened Belloc's arrival to an express train tearing through a quiet country station. "Old newspapers, paper bags and dust would be whirled frantically into the air and sucked along with the train for a few seconds. Then he would be gone and everything would settle into its habitual quiet."[13]

Belloc's temperament was essentially military. In 1891, while still a French citizen, he served in the French

Artillery at Toul – an experience that both reflected and reinforced his combative leanings. He cherished a life-long affection for the French Army, and was shocked by its ignominious collapse in 1940. He enjoyed writing on battles and wars, and during World War I was the chief military writer for the general public; producing a weekly column as well as several books, and setting forth his philosophy of history to an audience that would never have been reached by his more systematic historical studies.

Oxford

This background of military interest and propensity did not cease to be important even when Belloc left the army and entered Oxford University in 1892. Although he achieved a brilliant academic record, receiving a Brackenbury History Scholarship and taking First Class Honours in History in 1895, he found himself in an embattled environment. He failed to gain election to a Fellowship – a frustration that was always to gnaw at him, for he believed that such a post would have assured the financial security of his family, and provided the leisure and liberty with which to write the kind of books he really desired.

Belloc never forgot Oxford – in later years he would describe it as "a shrine, a memory, a tomb and a poignant possessing grief"[14] – and he always attributed his rebuff to anti-Catholic prejudice at the University. Whatever the reason, it seems unlikely that Belloc would actually have been happy there: his native restlessness and trenchant style would not have been at home in the comparatively passive and permissive atmosphere of academic life.

View of England

The outcome of his failure to gain a Fellowship was a growing sense of alienation from the English society of his adoption. Belloc was not only a Catholic in a predominantly Protestant culture, but a French European among English people, provincial in outlook and largely unaware of the wider traditions of Western culture. Thus a pugnacity of approach that was originally physical became also intellectual and social, and thereafter Belloc never departed from his attitude of fundamental opposition to the kind of society into which England had evolved.

He knew that such an attitude would never be easy to sustain. One must, he realised, be prepared "to perform the task and take wounds and loss as necessary parts of the struggle."[15] For his part he was propelled by a profound sense of duty and necessity, an unquenchable passion to proclaim the truth, whatever the cost.

Parliament

His years at Oxford had strengthened his resolve to play a part in English public life, and in 1906 he stood for Parliament as a Liberal candidate. Warned that his religion was a serious handicap, he rose to address a packed audience at his first public meeting, and began as follows:

> "Gentlemen, I am a Catholic. As far as possible, I go to Mass every day. This [taking a rosary out of his pocket] is a rosary. As far as possible, I kneel down and tell these beads every day. If you reject me on account of my religion, I shall thank God that He has spared me the indignity of being your representative."[16]

There was initial astonishment, followed by thunderous applause. Belloc was elected and served for almost five years. By temperament and upbringing he was a political radical of the Birmingham school – for his ancestry was English as well as French – and he believed deeply in the values of social freedom and reform. He also developed a lifelong distrust and dislike of the wealthy classes, and his egalitarian spirit could never abide the aristocratic domination of society. He held passionately to the necessity and value of the French Revolution, but he maintained that it was not the French side of his inheritance that nurtured this opposition to the rich. As he told the former editor of the London Tablet, Douglas Woodruff:

> "People think it was my French blood – because I have written about the French Revolution – that has made me against the rich, but it isn't – it is my Irish blood! A

Frenchman's instinct when he sees someone rich and powerful is to want to join him. But the Irishman more strongly wants to fight him."[17]

Belloc's experience of Parliament embittered him. He was affronted by the unashamed collusion and corruption that he saw, and distressed by the dwindling regard for common democratic liberties. He could not accept that, in political life, conviction is often tempered by compromise, and assertiveness by manoeuvre. When he left in 1910, he exclaimed acidly: "Perhaps they did not bribe me heavily enough, but in any case I am relieved to be quit of the dirtiest company it has ever been my misfortune to keep."[18]

Radical Social Philosopher

Belloc's most direct attack on the spurious state of modern parliamentary politics was a book he wrote with G.K. Chesterton's brother, Cecil, called *The Party System* (1911). This work alleged collusion between the two Front Benches in Parliament, so that genuine democratic representation and debate on matters of principle were no longer possible. Of more lasting importance, however, is his study of *The Servile State* (1912), a magisterial interpretation of political and social history. George Orwell judged this book to be prophetic, believing that it foretold "with remarkable insight the kind of things that have been happening from about 1930 onwards."[19]

Political commentary

Belloc's essential thesis was that our society is tending towards the condition of slavery which once characterised its social relations, and that the basis of the new slavery is a legal status involving compulsory labour. The present advantage of political freedom would not check this development, since it in turn depends on an economic freedom that results from the wide distribution of property ownership. Since capitalism centralises ownership in the hands of the few, thereby condemning the mass of citizens to insecurity and insufficiency, it is of its nature unstable.

The apparent alternative is socialism, but Belloc contended that this was not a solution to capitalism but rather its logical completion. The real solution was distributism, which would preserve social liberty by the restoration of private (and in general, family) ownership and power; re-establishing property as an institution normally integral to citizenship.

Distributism

Nearly a century has elapsed since Belloc enunciated his thesis of the *Servile State*, and the trend of events has amply justified his vision. Like all prophecies, the thesis itself is inexact in certain details; for example, it did not allow for the prodigious growth of bureaucratic control, since it assumed that social servility would be imposed by the capitalists, not by the State. Nonetheless, its central proposition – that social freedom is dependent on the decentralisation of power and the existence of widespread ownership – has gained increased if still limited acceptance, finding expression in such works as *Small Is Beautiful* (1973), a highly popular endorsement of distributist philosophy by E. F. Schumacher (1911-77).

Schumacher was an economist, a convert to Catholicism, who argued that technology should be adapted to the size and human needs of a given community, and that developing nations in particular should use technological products appropriate to their labour-intensive but impoverished circumstances. In addressing the problems of a technologised world and affirming the need for smaller devices and more manageable and personalised organisations, Schumacher countered the false impression that distributism necessarily involves a pastoral economy. This assumption was widely current in Belloc's time, and it must be admitted that his ideas were not applied sufficiently to the pressing contemporary problems of large-scale industry.

Influence in Australia

Belloc's social thought was far-reaching in its influence, perhaps especially in Australia where it carried a profound appeal for the Irish-Australian working-class radicalism that was energised in the 1930s by the publication of the *Catholic Worker*. Launched in Melbourne by a group of men nurtured by the Campion Society, this monthly paper used Belloc's analysis of the *Servile State* to explain the social condition of the times, and its first statement of principles was tersely Bellocian in flavour. The statement began: "We Fight."

Of special interest to the Australian people was the operation of minimum wage laws and compulsory arbitration, for these were listed by Belloc as among the signs of the Servile State. In a penetrating review of Belloc's thesis, the Australian historian, Fr James Murtagh, pointed out that the Australian arbitration system was not intrinsically servile; it had not involved the worker in compulsory labour on capitalist terms, but had exercised compulsion over the employer as well as the worker. He continued:

"The attempt to establish the rule of law in industrial relations by means of wage laws, trade union bargaining, arbitration and conciliation is in line with Christian social teaching and is the only approach to rebuilding social institutions in the atomised capitalist state. The only way the worker can acquire property – when he has not lost the sense and desire for it – is by means of a just wage. The only way the worker can regain status in society is through the trade union ... Finally, arbitration and conciliation between trade unions and employers' associations have not only greatly mitigated the evils of capitalism, but could be the first stage on the road back to the 'guild' principle in the form of joint industrial councils. And the restoration of the guild is an essential element in Belloc's sociological writings." [20]

The thesis of the Servile State was not an isolated segment of Belloc's thought. His mind was a remarkably integrated one, and he drew his sociology from the study of history, whose insights he applied to the broad problem of restoring a Christian humanist society.

Confronting anti-Catholic history

The separation of England from Christendom at the time of the Reformation had given rise to the Whig version of history, which was essentially Protestant in its interpretation and neglectful of the historical importance of the Catholic Church and the immense antiquity of the European tradition. Such a viewpoint affected the whole of English society and stood in the way of its return to the fullness of faith. It was Belloc's singular achievement – and his solitary destiny – to confront this social atmosphere and settled habit of thought that was hostile to Catholicism, and to transform it.

His influence was always social more than individual; collective rather than personal in its effects. Belloc did not convert a single mind here and there. Rather did he exercise, in Mgr. Ronald Knox's phrase, "a kind of hydraulic pressure on the thought of his age."[21] He made it impossible thereafter to disregard the historical significance of the Catholic Church or to scorn the values of the Catholic tradition. In the present-day context, where practices deeply offensive to the Christian conscience (like abortion) have received legal sanction, Belloc's approach and style afford an important insight into the dynamics of popular social change.

His success shows that it is not necessary, or even possible, to change the attitude of a whole society; only to change, by intellectual, social and political pressure, the respectable limits of behaviour that are supervised by the major opinion-formers (in particular the mass media).

Historical writings

Belloc's special historical interest was the Reformation, and he wrote variously on it – from narrative studies, like *How the Reformation Happened* (1928), to historical biographies, such as those of Wolsey and Cranmer. But he also undertook to write the whole history of England so that at every period the Whig bias might be corrected. Between 1925 and 1931 he published four volumes of a *History of England*, covering the period until 1612; and in 1934, a one-volume *Shorter History of England*. He had earlier produced a concluding volume to John Lingard's history, from 1689 to 1910. Only the years from 1612 to 1689 are nowhere treated in detail, but on this period he wrote biographies of Charles I, Oliver Cromwell, Charles II, James II, and Milton.

From the renowned French historian, Michelet (1798-1874), Belloc had learnt that "history should be a resurrection of the flesh."[23] To read Belloc's historical writings is indeed to feel the past come alive; to taste the full savour of another time; to be made aware of the continuity and creative promise of tradition.

Illustrative of this is his rousing conclusion on the fall of the monarchy in France:

"So perished the French monarchy. Its dim origins stretched out and lost themselves in Rome; it had already learnt to speak and recognised its own nature when the vaults of the Thermae echoed heavily to the slow footsteps of the Merovingian kings. Look up that vast valley of dead men crowned, and you may see the gigantic figure of Charlemagne, his brows level and his long white beard tangled like an undergrowth, having in his left hand the globe and in his right the hilt of an unconquerable sword. There also are the short, strong horsemen of the Robertian house, half-hidden by their leather shields, and their sons before them growing in vestment and majesty, and taking on the pomp of the Middle Ages; Louis VII, all covered with iron; Philip the Conqueror; Louis IX, who alone is surrounded with light: they stand in a widening interminable procession, this great crowd of kings; they loose their armour, they take their ermine on, they are accompanied by their captains and their marshals; at last, in their attitude and in their magnificence they sum up in themselves the pride and the achievement of the French nation."[24]

Belloc's chief study at Oxford had been English history, and he was keen to write an historical analysis of the roots of the Protestant Reformation in England. Yet his publisher insisted that, as he was half-French, his first historical works should be on two figures of the French Revolution, Danton and Robespierre. This had the effect of identifying Belloc in English eyes as basically French in his outlook and expertise, and in a sense as the apologist for a reign of terror, which at that time was the characteristic English historical judgement on the French Revolution. Certainly his experience at Oxford had shown him that this verdict was deficient. Belloc believed that, since the English Revolution had been made by the rich, the English found it hard to grasp the French Revolution, which had been made by the people. Thus, even in writing on this subject, he found himself in conflict with dominant opinion.

The Loneliness of a Personal Cross

Although combative by temperament, Belloc nevertheless
suffered intensely from the strain of combat, and he
regretted that the life of struggle and conflict, to which he
felt conscientiously called, prevented his sharing the
harmony and strength of common ways of thought. "We
are perpetually thrust into minorities," he lamented, "and
the world almost begins to talk a strange language."[24]

True witness

Above all in the matter of religion did Belloc feel an
intolerable sense of isolation. "I am abominably alone,"
he confessed in a letter to a friend. "I feel sometimes like
a sentry at night."[25] Yet he never shrank from the
necessity to bear witness, not only in the sense of moral
commitment, but also through a life of faithful conviction
and prayerful devotion. In a letter to Mgr. Knox in 1923,
he described the consequences of accepting such
a vocation:

"Those who bear witness do so at a vast and enduring
cost. It is an act of unique value and of proportionate
excellence and pain... It is a confirmation of the Faith
in others and in all, at the expense of one's own self. It

is the most real, enduring, and endless of the sacrifices. It is militant, expects nothing, and is paid at last in coin corresponding to its permanence of effect and magnitude of service. ... If emotion or rhetoric could determine the Divinity of Our Lord I should find it in the Agony and especially in the 'Eli, Eli.' That is the true note of the affair, and without it there is no witness. At least, so I think. It is a march in the night."[26]

Loving widower

Not only professional and social strain but personal tragedy intensified Belloc's sense of isolation and loneliness. In 1896 he married Elodie Hogan, whom he had loved at first sight when he met her in London six years before.[27] Their union was blessed with five children – three sons and two daughters. Unlike Belloc himself, who possessed a tough constitution, Elodie's health was always uncertain. In 1914 she died suddenly, and from the shock of her loss he never finally recovered. Her room was closed and never again used during Belloc's lifetime; and as he passed it on his way to bed, he would pause outside and trace upon the door the sign of the Cross. In later years, he was inclined to slip away from the enclosures of work and sit quietly in his wife's room; consoled yet saddened by the beauty of a life prematurely curtained. There he would remember – and there pray.

Further bereavement

In 1918 Belloc's eldest son, Louis, was killed in action on a bombing raid over Germany; and in 1941 his youngest son, Peter, died on active service in Scotland with the Royal Marines. Never for very long did Belloc escape the stabbing reminders of human mortality. His whole life, with its succession of disappointments and bereavements, was a battle, not only for the values – both natural and supernatural – of a cherished tradition, but even for survival itself. He was throughout a driven man, with a young family to raise and support and a hostile mental climate to combat and change.

Through every crisis it was his religious faith that ultimately preserved him. To Belloc, Catholicism was reality: "its whole point," he once declared, "is the facing of reality."[28]

Some years after his wife's passing, he wrote to a friend who was aggrieved by the death of her father:

"The advantage of the Faith in this principal trial of human life is that the Faith is Reality, and that through it all falls into a right perspective. That is not a consolation – mere consolation is a drug and to be despised – it is the strength of truth. We know how important life is (and no one knows that outside the Faith) but we also know that we are immortal and that those we love are immortal, and that the necessary condition, before eternity, is loss and change, and that we can regard them in the light of their final revelation and of reunion with what we love. I do not say this because I would make less the enormity of these blows. I know them as well as anyone and I reeled under them. But with the Faith they can be borne: they take on their right value. They are not final."[29]

The humorist

It might be imagined that Belloc was a morose and joyless man, totally subdued by the sad anxieties of a difficult life. Certainly he felt his burdens profoundly, as he testified in 1914 (soon after the death of his wife) in a letter to a friend who had lost his father:

"The business of human life turns, as I have heard that battles turn, not to tragedy but to agony towards the end. It has ultimate strains. And it is our business to lay ourselves against these strains with all our manhood. We are not allowed to break contact. Things of this kind must be endured, not passively, but with a sort of forward resistance... We suffer alone nearly always. We all die alone."[30]

Yet this was only one side of Belloc; it did not exhaust the depths of his personality. He was endowed with a rich capacity for humour and enjoyment – a love of creation

and a zest for life's gifts, both spiritual and temporal. At
their very first meeting, Chesterton had noticed this
exuberance of spirit in his friend, and realised that it
underlay his remarkable energy and courage.

Love of the countryside

Belloc bore a lifelong devotion to the land, and in
adolescence had entertained thoughts of becoming a
farmer. He had a keen sense of place, especially of rural
landscapes, and he was alive to the intimate relationship
between landscape and psychological experience. His
book, *The Four Men* (1912), explored this relationship
with great sensitivity, using the journey of four men
through the Sussex countryside as the occasion for
revealing the manifold aspects of his own nature. The
four men (Belloc himself, a poet, a sailor and a
philosopher) are, indeed, aspects of the author himself.

It was fitting that this pilgrimage (and *The Four Men*
naturally invites comparison with Belloc's other great
pilgrimage, *The Path to Rome*) should have taken place in
Sussex. At the age of seven his family had moved there
from London. When he married in 1896, he established
his own family in the same county, in a large house called
"Kings Land". It was to remain his home until his death
almost half a century later, and he grew to cherish it: "It
has my soul in it," he told a friend.[31]

Despite his trials and tragedies, Belloc never lost hold of what he called "the great lifebuoy of humour".[32] He not only produced works of humour – for example, the famous comic narrative poem, *The Modern Traveller* (1898), as well as a shelf of satirical novels – but his whole nature was threaded with a sense of fun and fellowship. Unquestionably, Belloc qualifies as a great "character", a man whose individuality was strong and unselfconscious.

His character

His grandson, the Benedictine Father, Philip Jebb, has provided a fascinating glimpse of the character of Belloc:

"He was always generous, and one felt that the habit of giving things to all and sundry had been deep-set in him all his life, even though it was coupled with a fine and violent strain of language and gesture when the Enemy was in sight – and there were plenty of enemies. A great day when he drove off with his blackthorn the platoon of soldiers who had started in the summer of 1940 to put up a barbed wire entanglement at the end of the vegetable garden beyond the Troll's Hut without first asking permission! And woe betide anyone (usually some unwary French-Canadian soldier from camp in the woods around Knepp Castle) if he was found sitting in Elodie Belloc's pew in the church at West Grinstead: he would get a sharp rap over the legs as he was driven forth with that ever-present blackthorn. Then would come the creaks and groans as he settled into his place and followed the Mass in an immense Roman missal (which must once have had its place on an altar), muttering the response half under his breath in those Tridentine days when only Dutch Modernists would have dreamt of a dialogue Mass."[33]

His behaviour in church was often amusing – and, for some, no doubt, embarrassing. In his own parish at West Grinstead, Sussex, he would periodically interrupt the priest reading out the notices by asking him in a loud voice which Sunday after Pentecost it happened to be. He was scrupulous about any debts he might have incurred, and on one occasion during Mass in Rouen Cathedral, he whispered piercingly to his friend, J.B. Morton (the famous humorist, "Beachcomber"): "I owe you fifty centimes on those last drinks."[34]

Love of the sea

Despite his tenacious faith and thrusting confidence, however, Belloc had a deeply restless spirit. At frequent intervals he felt the need for an activity that would provide both challenge and repose; at once reflect the insecurity of human life and relieve its immediate stresses. At such times he would turn to the sea.

For years he owned a thirty-foot cutter called the "Nona", in which he undertook many expeditions, at times crossing to France, at times sailing round a number of English capes. It was the latter kind of trip that he used as a framework for his book, *The Cruise of the "Nona"* (1925); for sailing along the English coast stimulated him to reminiscence and reflection on a range of subjects – history, literature, politics, religion, philosophy and controversy.

Belloc thought that the cruising of a boat is akin to the adventure of a human soul in a larger way: undertaken with purpose yet subject to innumerable diversions; aided by unforeseen blessings and opportunities yet troubled by terrible anxieties. Abroad on the sea provides the full model and symbol of human life, and thus the suitable setting for the chance thoughts of one human being; "For it is in the hours when he is alone at the helm, steering his boat along the shores, that a man broods most upon the past, and most deeply considers the nature of things."[35]

The Consummate Writer

The English poet, Sir John Squire, once remarked that "the man who attempts to survey the writings of Belloc will think he is undertaking to write the literary history of a small nation."[36]

Without doubt Belloc's literary output was both prodigious and versatile. He produced more than one hundred and fifty books as well as countless periodical articles. In a four-year period at the summit of his creative powers, 1906-1909, he published an historical biography; four volumes of essays (which had previously appeared in various journals); two satirical novels; two books of travel and topography; one volume of verse; and four pamphlets. Such diversity is astonishing, and it gives substance to Max Beerbohm's comment that Belloc "wasn't merely a man of genius; he was a man of many geniuses."[37] Though concentrated as a man, he was dispersed as a writer, and this has told against his reputation, since an age of specialism like our own finds it hard to admit mastery in more than one sphere.

Quality

Undeniably, Belloc ranks among the princes of modern English prose writers. He had a command of form and style, a sense of colour and rhythm, a feeling for the right word, and a flow of language resonant with the accents of speech. His prose is granite-like in its strength and simplicity. The literary critic, A.G. MacDonell, once compared Belloc's writing to a symphonic movement:

> "The flute, the artillery trumpet, the lovely cadences of the violin, the angry clash of the cymbal and the thunder of the organ, all are contained in that magic pen. And the knowledge of a lifetime, in Whistler's immortal phrase, is poured out through this great and unorthodox orchestra of prose."

Path to Rome

Numberless passages illustrate the beauty of Belloc's writing, but a particularly memorable sample can be found in *The Path to Rome*, the book that is still, perhaps, most readily associated with Belloc's name:

> "I have waited for the dawn a hundred times, attended by that mournful, colourless spirit which haunts the last hours of darkness; and influenced especially by the great timeless apathy that hangs round the first uncertain promise of increasing light. For there is an hour before daylight when men die, and when there is nothing above the soul or around it, when even the stars fail. And this long and dreadful expectation I had thought to be worst when one was alone at sea in a

small boat without wind; drifting beyond one's
harbour in the ebb of the outer channel tide, and
sogging back at the first flow on the broad, confused
movement of a sea without any waves. In such lonely
mornings I have watched the Owers light turning, and
I have counted up my gulf of time, and wondered that
moments could be so stretched out in the clueless
mind. I have prayed for the morning or for a little
draught of wind, and this I have thought, I say, the
extreme of absorption into emptiness and longing."[37]

In *The Path to Rome*, Belloc recounted his experiences
and moods during a long pilgrimage on foot from Toul to
Rome, culminating in his arrival at St. Peter's for High
Mass on the Feast of Sts Peter and Paul.

Throughout the years, the book has been read and
revered, and the very title has become a commonplace in
the vocabulary of Catholic conversion. Sir Arnold Lunn,
who always attested that it was Belloc's influence which
first set his own feet on "the path to Rome", believed that
the fading of memory in old age was not without its
consolations: it made the re-reading of *The Path to Rome*
an agreeable necessity every year!

The book itself escapes easy classification. It is a
chronicle of moods and of memories, a celebration of the
author's deepest citizenship, which was above all
religious, but also cultural; Catholic, but also European.

When the author first saw the Alps, he was moved to express the faith that had inspired his pilgrimage:

> "From the height of Weissenstein I saw, as it were, my religion ... The great peaks made communion between that homing creeping part of me which loves vineyards and dances and a slow movement among pastures, and that other part which is only properly at home in Heaven ... These, the great Alps, seen thus, link one in some way to one's immortality."[39]

The Path to Rome brought back to English literature a realisation of the cultural heritage of Europe. Belloc's great gift of visual imagery and his sense of the presence of the past enabled him to evoke the Western tradition in a most powerful and picturesque way. In his mind, the spiritual and the cultural were intimately intertwined, and the cultural history of Europe had about it a spiritual power of resurgence. It is the quality of Western Europe, he observed in one essay, "ever to transform itself but never to die."[40] Its cultural energies were quickened by religious faith, and Belloc was always moved when this process gave rise to the plenitude of a Catholic culture.

Catholic Church

At one stage on his journey, he passed through a village in Switzerland. He saw all the people pouring into the church and begin to sing psalms. The spectacle was a sudden sign of a religiously united culture – and a poignant reminder of the Europe that now lay divided:

"At this [sight] I was very much surprised, not having been used at any time of my life to the unanimous devotion of an entire population, but having always thought of the Faith as something fighting odds... My whole mind was taken up and transfigured by this collective act, and I saw for a moment the Catholic Church quite plain, and I remembered Europe and the centuries."[41]

This deep sense of affinity with the European past was not widely evident among English-speaking people in Belloc's time. The Whig view of history prevented any positive grasp of cultural continuity, for it ignored the contribution of the Catholic Church. Belloc was always astounded at the extent and depth of ignorance that prevailed concerning the Church. As Robert Speaight observed:

"Here, [Belloc] would say, was the thing which had determined the destiny of Europe; the thing recognised, even when it was hated, by every educated man or woman on the continent; the thing which had to be taken into account in deciding any large issue of politics or morals. And yet it was persistently ignored by the finest intelligences of the country he had made his own... So long as he had breath in his body he would try to explain to people what it meant to belong to a living, teaching and continuing Church."[42]

A sacramental faith

Belloc's conception of the Catholic Church was Roman in emphasis, just as his approach to religion itself was sacramental and institutional. In a book of reflections on North Africa, *Esto Perpetua* (1906), he relates the story of the French commander who wanted to engrave the number of his regiment on a slab of mountain rock, only to find that a Roman officer had recorded the presence of his soldiers long before. Belloc's sense of the European past was shaped and sharpened by his love of Rome in its pre-Christian as well as Christian phase. He was ever conscious of what he termed "that tenacious chain of antiquity,"[43] and he saw the Church very much as the heir of pagan Rome; an institution which had absorbed the values and traditions of classical culture and carried on the universal mission of the Roman Empire at a new and more exalted level.

Religion was never vague or abstract to Belloc: it was concrete and cultural. He was possessed of a strong sacramental sense and he recognised the immense importance of institutional support and stimulation in the matter of religious faith. He was not by nature a devout or spiritually impulsive person, nor was he an instinctive moraliser. His make-up was philosophical and cultural, formed by a logical mind and a broad social experience. His attention was focused, not chiefly upon commitment but upon faithfulness; not primarily upon morality but upon the hard core of belief and doctrine which gives morality its foundation and validity. He was intellectually convinced of the truth of Catholicism, but he realised, in company with most ordinary people, that he could not rely on the emotional experience of faith to sustain him. As he admitted on one occasion:

> "I have no spiritual experience myself: or so little that I cannot weigh it. But I know and see that the Church is the salvation of mankind, and of the family and of the individual: politically and socially and in the private character it is all. Therefore to have played one's part in the establishment and maintenance of it, especially in the difficult outposts – is much more than duty done: it is glory and the unrecognised beginning of beatitude."[44]

The greatest saints and mystics enjoyed the experience of God without any aid from the senses. But, said Belloc:

> "I cannot boast myself to be of such a kind, and on my own poor level it is landscape, the sea, human love, music, and the rest, that help to make me understand: and in their absence I am very empty indeed."[45]

Catholic advocate

As a Catholic advocate, Belloc covered a vast and varied
field. His output included not only history and culture,
but also politics and sociology, for he understood the
wide impact of religious belief on human affairs. His
most significant works, like *Europe and the Faith* (1920)
and *Survivals and New Arrivals* (1929), unfold certain
key ideas – such as the means by which Catholicism
conquered the mind and heart of pagan antiquity and
became the vitalising root of Western civilisation; the fact
that this extension of the Incarnation in time was the
result of a Church – a body, not merely a belief, an
institution, not only a faith; the realisation that the
dismemberment of the Church and the dissolution of a
Catholic people would bring about the re-paganisation of
society and a new night of despair.

Belloc has been charged with identifying the Church
too completely with Europe and with the Latin genius that
developed but did not create the Faith. There is little doubt
that he did indeed minimise the Jewish contribution to
Christianity and the importance of the Faith outside
Europe (in the Middle East and elsewhere). In these
respects he was bound by the intellectual limitations of his
time and his own background; but his overriding aim was
to correct the neglect of a central force in Western culture
– the Catholic Church – and thus his work partakes of the
achievements and oversights of the pioneer.

Yet there remains no doubt that Belloc's precursory efforts secured a more sympathetic reception for the stylistically tamer if more finely balanced treatises of Catholic historians like Christopher Dawson. As Mr T.M. Butler wrote in an Australian tribute to Belloc:

"He was in many ways a litigant in history, contending as an advocate against the biased contentions of the Whig theory of history. Out of the clamour of Belloc versus Whig has emerged much that has assisted later historians in their more scientific and more objective historical judgements."[46]

Apologetics

Belloc was always aware that apologetics was not a mere matter of extolling the historical triumphs of the Church. It was, pre-eminently, the challenge of demonstrating the Church's divine capacity to answer the critical questions of human existence. As he asked:

"Does [man] only mature, grow old and die, or is that process but part of a larger destiny? Have his actions permanent or only ephemeral consequences to himself? Are awful unseen powers to which he devotes gratitude, worship and fear, imaginations of his or real? Are his dead no longer in being? Is he responsible to a final Judge?"[47]

Such questions are fundamental – and Belloc proposed the Church as the only authentic answer to them. "What is the Catholic Church?", he asked in a noble and oft-quoted open letter to W. R. Inge, the Dean of St Paul's Cathedral in London:

"It is that which replies, co-ordinates, establishes. It is that within which is right order; outside, the puerilities and the despairs. It is the possession of perspective in the survey of the world. It is a grasp upon reality. Here alone is promise, and here alone a foundation."[48]

An Enduring Legacy

Few tasks are more difficult than to reanimate departed fame, and in Belloc's case the difficulty is intensified by the kind of writing in which he engaged. His prime purpose was to teach – to form people's minds and often also to change them; and thus it is not easy to separate his gifts from his views, or to give a precise estimate of his life and legacy. The literary critic, Frank Swinnerton, has predicted that a century will pass before Belloc's gifts are fully realised and acknowledged; and then "his genius will shine like the jewel it is."[49]

Dedicated to his apostolate

The resurgence of Belloc's reputation would seem to rest chiefly on a revival of sympathetic interest in historic Catholicism, and in the Western civilisation that has so far formed its most complete expression. To these causes Belloc gave himself unstintingly, knowing all the time that public judgement was as likely to scorn his efforts as it did those of the French poet and political activist, Paul Déroulède (1846-1914). Belloc may well have discerned the parallel with himself when he wrote:

"Déroulède hammered away all his life at the expense of ceaseless insult and contempt, paying for the preservation of his honour the heavy price of an unbroken isolation, and dying without seeing any apparent fruit of his effort." [50]

Skilled poet

Not only did Belloc pursue his apostolate without public acclaim, but he knew that such work kept him from engaging seriously in a form of writing which might well have clinched his literary reputation – namely, poetry. He wrote mainly in prose because that was the appropriate weapon for combat, but he never lost his yearning to be remembered by posterity as a poet. His first published works were verse, most notably *The Bad Child's Book of Beasts* (1896) and *More Beasts (for Worse Children)* (1897), comic verse which has enchanted a great many nurseries since its publication; and he produced at different times a modicum of verse, both light and serious, culminating in a long and painstakingly composed work, *The Heroic Poem in Praise of Wine* (1932). But the bugle-call to apostolic action sounded unceasingly for Belloc, and he could never linger long in what he called, in one poem, "my rightful garden."[51]

Intellectual courage

Belloc built his life round the necessity to affirm truths that are important, "even those which seem, to others, at their first statement mere nonsense"; for he believed that "reality will in time confirm your effort."[52] He himself shouldered a heavy sense of failure – and yet he never gave up. He was a man of immense character and courage, particularly of that rare kind – intellectual courage. Indeed, in large measure, his vocation was that of an intellectual martyr; and no martyr ultimately fails. In the memory of Douglas Woodruff, "the final impression is one of great integrity, of a man who never wrote anything that he did not believe ... He was a true man through and through."[53]

The greatness of Belloc may still be measured by those who read his prose or verse and gain access to a luminous mind and a kindling character. He himself framed his own epitaph in verse:

"He does not die that can bequeath
Some influence to the land he knows."[54]

The influence of Belloc may still be felt – in a steady deepening of fidelity or a sudden rush of realism; in a summoning of courage or a call to courtesy. It may still be active in a renewed capacity to live with disappointment and the terrible ache of loneliness; in a surge of passionate anger against manifest evil; or in a willingness to stand alone for what is right in face of antagonism and unpopularity.

The spirit of Belloc may still be captured in the thunder of a voice swift to bear witness, and the silence of a heart sworn to sacrifice; in the strength of a self-confident stride, and in the humility of a face lowered in prayer.

It is no shallow spirit or insignificant influence – and it is no small legacy.

Further reading

While Hilaire Belloc has not enjoyed the posthumous attention which his fellow Catholic writer, G.K. Chesterton, has received - as measured by the number of critical studies and reprints of his works - there have been several important biographies published; in particular, A.N. Wilson's *Hilaire Belloc* (1984) and Joseph Pearce's *Old Thunder: A Life of Hilaire Belloc* (2002). The official biography of him, *The Life of Hilaire Belloc* (1957), by Robert Speaight, remains a significant and finely crafted portrait of the man.

A recent study of importance is a chapter on Belloc in Ian Ker's *The Catholic Revival in English Literature, 1845-1961* (2003), in which Belloc is thoughtfully related to other important writers of the Catholic literary renaissance in recent centuries, in particular Newman and Chesterton.

Belloc's social and political criticism has continued to attract critical attention, and a number of his books, including *Essay on the Restoration of Property* (2002) and *The Free Press* (2002), have been republished by IHS Press of Norfolk, Virginia (USA) - see *www.ihspress.com*

In England, a Hilaire Belloc Society was established in 1997 to promote interest in his life and works. Its journal, "*The Bellocian*," edited by Dr Grahame Clough, has provided an invaluable source of elusive secondary material. For further information, readers can contact the Society at: *HilaireBelloc1@Aol.com*

An American Belloc Society was formed in 2005, and its Washington DC-based Director is Scott J. Bloch.

Endnotes

1   "Hilaire Belloc" in P. Caraman (ed.), *Occasional Sermons of Ronald A. Knox,* 1960, p.410.

2   On both of the Belloc anniversaries, conferences and other celebrations were held in England and elsewhere – for example, in 1970, at Spode House in Rugeley, Staffordshire (see "Belloc 70," *Spode House Review*, August 1972), and the Catholic Stage Guild held a centenary tribute in music and speech in London involving Sir Ralph Richardson and other notable actors; while in 2003, a conference took place at Plater College, Oxford and another, "Belloc revisited," in Sydney at Campion College Australia, and various articles appeared (such as Paul Ross, "Warrior for the Faith," *Catholic Herald* (London), 20th June 2003, p.7, and Tony Evans, "Celebrating Hilaire Belloc," *Annals Australia*, July 2003, pp.30-2).

3   *An Open Letter on the Decay of Faith*, 1906, p.12.

4   F.J. Sheed, "Belloc the Apologist," *The Tablet* (London), 25th July 1953, p.82.

5   *The Advocate* (Melbourne), 18th August 1955, p.9.

6   Christopher Hollis, Foreword to *Hilaire Belloc's Prefaces, written for fellow authors.* Selected by J.A. de Chantigny. 1971. pp.24-5.

7   Based on a description by Robert Speaight, "Hilaire Belloc," *The Month* (London), September 1953, p.140.

8   Quoted by Robert Speaight, "On Writing the Biography of Hilaire Belloc," *Twentieth Century* (Melbourne), Spring 1957, p.11.

9   Bernard Levin, "Pantomime Horse," *Spectator* (London), 5th December 1958, pp.833-4.

10 *Letters of Hilaire Belloc*, 1958, p.274.

11 *Catholic Herald* (London), 24th July 1970.

12 Marie Belloc Lowndes, *I, too, have lived in Arcadia*, 1942, p.214.

13 Robert Speaight, *Life of Hilaire Belloc*, 1957, p.513.

14 *Letters*, 1958, p.260.

15 *Ibid.,* p.115.

16 Speaight, *op.cit.*, p.204.

17 Douglas Woodruff, "The Radical and the Catholic," *Spode House Review*, August 1972, p.21

18 Speaight, *op.cit.*, pp.295-6.

19 George Orwell, "Second thoughts on James Burnham," *Collected Essays*, 1961, p.371.

20 J.G. Murtagh, " 'The Servile State' – Forty Years Later," *Twentieth Century* (Melbourne), Spring 1953, p.44.

21 "Hilaire Belloc," in Caraman, *op.cit.*, p.413.

22 Speaight, *op.cit.*, p.134.

23 *Danton: A Study*, 1899, p.206.

24 *The Path to Rome*, 1902, p.159.

25 Speaight, *op.cit.*, p.245.

26 *Ibid.,* pp.147-8.

27 A most interesting study of Belloc's relationship with Elodie Hogan is Marylyn Whitrow, "Belloc in Love," *Illustrated London News*, Christmas Number 1980, p.42.

28 *World Conflict* (London: CTS), 1953, p.5.

29 *Letters,* 1958, p.191.

30 *Ibid.*, pp.61-2.

31 *Ibid.*, p.164.

32 *Ibid.*, p.248.

33 Philip Jebb, "Hilaire Belloc as a Grandfather," *Downside Review*, October 1970, p.342-3.

34 J.B. Morton, *Hilaire Belloc*: A Memoir, 1955, p.135.

35 *Cruise of the "Nona"* , 1925, p.xxxvi.

36 Speaight, *op.cit.*, p.xiii.

37 *Ibid.*, p.255.

38 *The Path to Rome*, 1902, p.364.

39 *Ibid.*, p.180.

40 "Jose Maria de Heredia," *First and Last,* 1911, p.147.

41 *The Path to Rome*, 1902, p.157-8.

42 Robert Speaight, "Hilaire Belloc," *The Month* (London), September 1953, p.138.

43 *Many Cities*, 1928, p.207.

44 *Letters,* 1958, p.248.

45 *Many Cities*, p.247.

46 T.M. Butler, "Hilaire Belloc – A Tribute," *Catholic Worker* (Melbourne), July 1970, p.4. A salient example of Belloc's influence is the revised interpretation of the 16th century Reformation in recent decades. Scholarly works that are more favourable to the Catholic Church, such as J. J. Scarisbrick's *The Reformation and the English Peoples* (1984) and Eamon Duffy's *The Stripping of the Altars* (1992), would have arguably been more difficult to publish had not Belloc helped to demolish the wall of anti-Catholic prejudice that had secured the prevailing Protestant understanding of this major historical episode.

47 *Survivals and New Arrivals*, 1929, p.232.

48 "A Letter to Dean Inge," *Essays of a Catholic Layman in England*, 1931, pp.304-5.

49 Frank Swinnerton, *The Georgian Literary Scene 1910-1935*, rev.ed.1969, p.7.

50 *The Cruise of the "Nona"* , 1925, p.52.

51 "Stanzas Written on Battersea Bridge during a South-Westerly Gale," *Sonnets & Verse*, 1923, p.56.

52 *The Cruise of the "Nona"* , p.51.

53 Douglas Woodruff, "Belloc, Man of Integrity," *The Month* (London), July 1970, p.23.

54 *The Four Men: A Farrago,* 1912, p.309.